W9-BWE-948

THE SURE VICTORY

Madame Chiang Kai-shek

THE SURE VICTORY

FLEMING H. REVELL COMPANY

Printed in the United States of America

LIBRARY OF CONGRESS CATALOG CARD NUMBER: 55–11697

Westwood, N.J.—316 Third Avenue
London E.C. 4—29 Ludgate Hill
Glasgow C. 2—219 Bothwell Street

THE SURE VICTORY

信

I had great hesitancy about writing this message, for several reasons. One is that I do not want to give the impression that I am a better Christian than I am. After considerable thought I came to the conclusion that no one who has had a unique experience with prayer has a right to withhold it from others. Besides, I believe that the main line of attack against the evils of today is in my hands and in yours—in prayer.

Some five years ago I started a small prayer group here on Formosa. I have seen results that defy reasoning. I deeply feel that enough prayer groups of men, women, and children, praying to God for His guidance, will bring about manifestations of power beyond ordinary hopes.

The Communists preach a doctrine of brotherly love that takes action in enslavement and tyranny. They promote the nonexistence of God.

In less than a dozen years they have conquered with comparatively little of their own blood, between seven and eight hundred million people and some thirty-seven million square kilometers of territory in different parts of the world.

We Christians believe in the love of God and in the brotherhood of men under the Fatherhood of God. But we have comparatively little to show toward its accomplishment. Why?

The chief difference, I venture to say, is that the dedicated Communists hold fanatically to their belief and work with disciplined fervor while most of us nominal Christians have become watered down and weak-kneed in faith, and flaccid with lassitude.

Many people say they would do anything to have real lasting world peace. But will they try the simple experiment of prayer?

Through our own experiences in prayer I am convinced that a chain of prayer groups around the world will be more powerful than any propaganda.

In order that you may understand why I think so, I must first give you a short sketch of the events and circumstances that have shaped my thinking.

My own spiritual road has been slow and painful. The soul, in making its Pilgrim's Progress, reaches a crisis and falters. Often these are times when it seems impossible to pray at all. Spiritual readings seem prosaic and platitudinous. Everything goes wrong. Then come irritation, pique, indecision, sleeplessness, and ineffectualness. There follow waves of resentment, anger, grievance, a sense of futility, and a feeling of failure. Yet if we can persist in praying, we are bound to rise to a sturdier effort and a sense of joyous calm. A Truth is clearer.

Both my parents were devout Christians and we were

brought up with religious training. Even as little children we had to attend Sunday school and church and observe daily family devotions. As is usual in such cases, I sometimes rebelled against this rigorous schedule. Most of my friends could play all day Sunday while I had to sit quietly and listen to tedious sermons and prayers. Nevertheless, and without conscious effort, I absorbed Christian ideals. Yet even after my marriage I was merely a nominal Christian.

Perhaps I should explain a little further what I mean by a nominal Christian. In my mind I accepted unquestioningly and unreservedly the divinity of Christ, His teachings and His grace. I believed, too, that Jesus came to the world to atone for sinners, but frankly this meant little to me. Although He died for me, He also died for everybody. This fact, therefore, had no personal significance. It was like enjoying a cool breeze on a hot summer day. Everybody enjoyed it who felt it. The breeze was nothing personal; it was just there. I was grateful for it but not inordinately so. As far as being a sinner was concerned, everybody was a sinner and certainly my sins were no more wicked than those of the average person. This is what I mean by acceptance in my mind, instead of a truly personal experiencing of faith.

I knew that my mother felt differently, but I merely thought that she was overly religious. I recognized that Mother lived very close to God and that she was a great soul. She spent hours praying and communing with Him. Whenever we had problems, we would go to her and ask her to pray for us. She repeatedly told us that we ourselves should pray. What is more, she would not be hurried with God. By experience we learned that she could pray us through anything. Whenever our problems were solved, we forgot her wondrous intercession until the next time, but she did not. She would start devotions of thanksgiving.

To Mother, praying to God was not merely asking Him to bless her children. It meant waiting on Him. With her religion was not a one-way street. She lived according to His precepts to do justly, to love mercy, and to walk in spirit humbly with Him. She often emphasized to me that we should not ask God's help if the request would hurt someone else.

I can see her now, quite ill, a few months before her death. She had an unusually active mind and was greatly concerned about the nation. The year of 1931 was a memorable year in more ways than one to me. It was the year that the Japanese renewed and enlarged their aggressive program against China in the now famous Mukden Incident of September, and the tell-tale traces of the hand of aggression could already be detected earlier in the year. One day while talking to her, a thought which I considered quite bright occurred to me.

"Mother, you are so powerful in prayer, why don't you pray to God to destroy Japan in an earthquake so that she can no longer harm China?"

She turned her face away from me, and then replied: "Don't ask me to pray to God to do anything that is unworthy even of you, a mortal. *Vengeance is mine, saith the Lord.** It certainly isn't yours."

Her death in June 1931 was a terrific blow to all her children, but it hit me perhaps even harder than the rest, for I was

* Romans 12:19.

her youngest daughter and had leaned on her more heavily than I realized. At that time, in addition to the ever-increasing Japanese encroachment, my husband had the added burden of suppressing the Communists, then rampant in the province of Kiangsi. Floods had overrun the dikes of the Yellow River, and a large section of our people were threatened by famine. Discouragement close to despair overwhelmed me, and Mother was no longer there to pray me through my personal as well as other troubles. I had a lifetime to face without her. What was I to do? To whom could I turn?

In retrospect, I realize that this was my first great spiritual crisis.

I looked around and found that my husband was being faithful to the promise that he had made to my mother before our marriage, to study the Bible. Although she had converted him to Christianity just before her death, he was still studying daily by himself, trying to understand the complexities of Old Testament history. It was tedious work and seemingly unrewarding, for there were few comprehensive Chinese biblical histories which made sense to one who was not brought up a Christian. When I saw him struggling, I knew I should help him as Mother always had.

Years back, while attending Wellesley College in the United States, (after finishing high school at Wesleyan), I had taken a course in Old Testament History. In those days almost all colleges required at least one year of Bible study if only for the purpose of acquainting the students with the finest writing on record. But the Bible was blood and bone of the American homesteaders who settled the land, and it became part and parcel of their cultural foundation. Perhaps I, as a foreigner, could see more clearly than my American schoolmates how closely the make-up of the country had followed the principles of Christianity. Somewhat vaguely, I connected God's abundant blessing of America whatever its foibles and sins, with the keeping of the Lord's teaching.

Wellesley's was a systematic course, giving a comprehensive outline of biblical times. How strange that years later that course should prove so useful in the enlightenment of the Generalissimo! Now I could utilize what I had learned, and with some of my old notes and textbooks help my husband with his Bible studies.

Oftentimes I believe God has a plan in minutiae and we do not see the pattern until years later. The daily session between the Generalissimo and myself, which started out to be devotional, has come to be a source of common strength and an integral part of our lives. Every morning since then, at six-thirty, we have prayed together and have shared devotional reading and dicussion. Every night before retiring, we also pray together.

As my own faith has grown through meditations and fresh understanding, a deeper meaning has come of our prayers together. Many a time a feeling of spiritual peace seems to exude from within me, bringing completely annihilated self, with the mind in quiet and continuous absorption in the keen contemplation of God. When in this state, one is practically oblivious to the calls of this world, likes and dislikes, honor and name, hate and love.

I knew that I had reached the first plateau of my spiritual development.

The habit of daily morning devotions proved to be a rock of sustaining strength to my husband when he was taken captive in Sian in 1936 by some of his officers who were secretly in league with the Communists. Despite dire mental distress and a physical injury from a fall when he was captured, he was spiritually at peace as a prisoner, although death faced him at any moment. His captors held him incommunicado for ten days while newspapers of the world reported his plight in bannerlines, and the nation clamored for his return to safety.

A few days previous to his capture, I was in Loyang with him to celebrate his fiftieth birthday. There illness forced me to fly to Shanghai to see my doctor, while the Generalissimo went to Sian. It was in Shanghai, therefore, that I first learned of his capture. On the same night I made haste for Nanking, the Capital, where the ideas and opinions of responsible people on how to deal with the situation conflicted with one another.

Finally, I succeeded in flying to Sian to be at his side. When his captors conducted me to him, he was as startled as though I were an apparition. Recovering from his surprise, he showed me a verse in the Bible which he had read that same morning: "The Lord has created a new thing on the earth: a woman protects a man."*

I do not intend to convey here the impression that I could literally protect him from the imminent physical danger that existed. In fact, by flying to his side I had exposed myself to share

* Jeremiah 31:22, R.S.V.

his fate, whatever that might be. The remarkable thing is that I think God, through the Bible, used these words as a signal to convey to him the double message of "*All is right,*" and my impending arrival in Sian.

Is it any wonder that he and I should believe so strongly in the power of prayer?

I reached the next plateau of spiritual growth during the Sino-Japanese War in 1937. Perhaps the greatest migration in history was the trek of the Chinese people, following the Old Silk Route, to set up a new Capital in the interior. Chungking was in the remote, rocky, cavernous region of Szechuan province, fourteen hundred miles from the coast, through mountains and gorges. We moved everything. We moved whatever we could of our factories. We moved our arsenals and all available machinery. We even marched our Jersey and Guernsey cows from Nanking. We used every conveyance imaginable: trucks, rickshas, wheelbarrows, litters, palanquins, sedan-chairs, carts, and the human back.

Most of the people who migrated and fled from the enemy had never seen Szechuan. Not only to the world but to most of the migrants, Szechuan province was almost a legendary name. Situated at the end of the famous Yangtze Gorges, it is a fabulous place for many kinds of medicinal herbs, the scenic mountain of Omei with its Buddhist temples and monasteries, the natural gas cum salt well of Tse-Liu-Tsing, and the home of the pandas. There, too, are the still usable Kwanhsien Canals, one of the greatest engineering feats in the world, built some two thousand years ago; and, at one time, before the National Government had extended its real authority over it, it was the home bed of the poppies.

Since the Communists have taken over the mainland in 1949, unhappily for China and the world, this area has again become the source of narcotics from which opium is being deliberately, systematically, and covertly grown, in turn to be made into heroin and morphine, and distributed to weaken the moral stamina and poison physically and spiritually the youths and soldiers of Asia, Europe, Africa, and the Americas.

In the Southwestern provinces with Szechuan province as the orbit, we set up homes and government as the base of national resistance against the foreign invader. Here our people lived in nightmares of privations and bombings for seven years.

For the first few years and especially in 1939 and 1940, bombers came by day and by bright moonlight, in seemingly never-ending waves of death. Sometimes they came round the clock. Here we lived in underground shelters almost as much as we lived above ground. The makeshift dugouts, without the equipment to regulate air, were terribly damp and fetid because of sweating porous stones and water dripping from the sides of the caves. Other air-raid shelters were stuffy from dead air and stench. And so, except for moments when each wave of planes was directly overhead, I, for one, to minimize the rheumatic pains brought on by humid surroundings, would leave the dugouts for the open air. On bright moonlight nights, to forget the misery and the fatigue, I sometimes played games with my ever-faithful secretary.

I knew that to dwell on what the enemy was doing to my

country caused me such resentment and hate that mentally and physically I was like a top, winding ever more taut and which, when the momentum is spent, will surely fall.

For over a year, whenever in a dugout, to keep my mind from misery and low morale brought on by physical fatigue and illness, I practiced conversational French with a kind-hearted Belgian priest. Once so many waves of enemy planes bombed Chungking that we were in the dugout for the greater part of the day. Toward nightfall, I said to Father Weitz, "Let us continue our lesson outside." Presently the emergency alert again sounded and my husband called to me to return to the bomb shelter. Just as we got in the passageway, the bowels of the earth seemed to be torn asunder from the concussion of the bomb dropped near the spot where we had sat. We were pitched forward flat on our faces, and our bodies were covered with a shower of earth and rubble. The French grammar book which I had been studying was sliced clear through by a piece of shrapnel.

To some, the fact that I was not killed seemed just a lucky escape. To others, and my husband and I among them, it was further proof of God's design in one's life.

Every time we came out of the dugouts we faced a worse condition. The city of Chungking is situated on a tongue of land at the juncture of two rivers, the Chialing and the Yangtze. Steep stone steps lace their way up and down the hillsides and the old houses were built in such a way that there was only one entrance. Oftentimes when a bomb exploded and cut off the one entrance the householders would be trapped without any means of egress.

Whole sections of the city were turned into shambles by a few bombs, as the houses were so closely grouped together that one incendiary bomb set a whole block afire. We knew days when it was impossible to obtain coffins, as the toll of death mounted.

In time, all the business section of the city was demolished, so that it was possible to stand in the middle of the city and get an unobstructed view of the rivers on both sides. It is to the credit of our people that they were uncowed, for after each bombing, scarcely had the all-clear siren trailed off its last thin echo before the surviving householders returned to their burned shops and homes and began to salvage whatever they could. A few days later, temporary shacks and buildings would make their appearance on the old sites.

Some days the raids were so close and numerous that no one had time to prepare food. Hours were wasted in the dugouts—valuable hours needed for work and rest. Moonlight nights were the worst, for the marauding planes, timed with devilish guile, came in successive waves. Terrible tiredness permeated nerve and bone; it seemed preferable to risk being bombed to death than to seek safety.

We knew that the enemy was trying to break our morale through sheer physical exhaustion. Therefore, all the more we were inflexible in our resolve not to give in. No greater tribute could be paid to our sorely tried people than this: that in all their sufferings never did they complain against their leaders. Never did they falter in the determination that the enemy must be driven from our shores.

Determination and will power, however, are quite different

from the power that comes from faith and prayer. About the third year of living half-underground with my aggravated condition of neuro-dermatitis, I came to a new point of spiritual desolation. I said my prayers and they meant nothing. They were just words. I realized that I was being slowly poisoned by resentment, hate, and bitterness.

Did you ever try to pray for an enemy? Have you ever tried to love someone who is ruining your life? I knew what the teaching of Christ was, but I could not follow it. I could not ask blessings for the aggressors no matter how I tried. Surely even God could not demand that of me!

Then after one of our morning devotions, when the bombing was particularly intense, I happened to recall a certain experience. My husband and I, on one of our trips to the front, had stayed in a house next to an orphanage for blind children. When they heard that I was next door, they asked me to visit them. Though I hated the instinctive tendency in myself, I have always been repulsed by abnormality, whether mental or physical. Yet I went, of course, as a matter of duty. As I entered their school, the expressions on some of the faces of the children seemed unnervingly dull and apathetic. Never had I realized so clearly that the eyes are the windows of the soul. These poor sightless ones seemed to lack not only windows but souls. I fought hard against an impulse to push them away and to flee.

Then this thought flashed through my mind which just as suddenly made me want to embrace these children. If I am so repulsed by physical blindness and defacement, how much more repulsed must God be by my spiritual blindness and ugliness? And our spiritual blindness is often willful and determined.

Recalling that incident at morning devotions, I asked myself whether I was not spiritually blind deliberately when I hated. Then my ears seemed to echo my mother's voice, saying: "*Vengeance is mine, saith the Lord.* It certainly isn't yours." Thus I was enabled to unload my hate at the foot of the Cross. Now when I pray I can turn the enemy over to God, His mercy, and His justice.

Many people have spoken with special warmth of a speech that I made in Madison Square Garden, New York City, in 1943. Few knew of the inner struggle I had to go through before I could say the following words and mean them with all my heart:

"There must be no bitterness in the reconstructed world. No matter what we have undergone and suffered, we must try to forgive those who injured us and remember only the lesson gained thereby.

"The teachings of Christ radiate ideas for the elevation of souls and intellectual capacities far above the common passions of hate and degradation. He taught us to help our less fortunate fellow-beings, to work and strive for their betterment without ever deceiving ourselves and others by pretending that tragedy and ugliness do not exist. He taught us to hate the evil in men, but not men themselves.

"Selfishness and complacency in the past have made us pay dearly in terms of human misery and suffering. While it may be difficult for us not to feel bitterness for the injuries we have suffered at the hands of the aggressors, let us remember that recrimination and hatred will lead us nowhere."

In realizing my own spiritual blindness and God's mercy, hatred could never again obsess or rule me. I still get angry, but that is a momentary reaction. No bitterness goes so deep within me as to possess my every thought and render my actions futile.

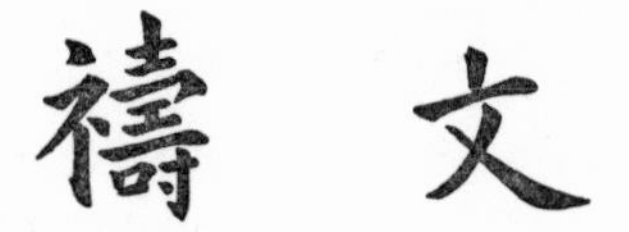

Nothing mental or spiritual ever stands still. There is need periodically for renewed progress; without it we retrogress. These are the times when so many Christians lose their faith and fall away by the roadside. But to those who persist in earnest prayers, seeking enlightenment from God, there will come a fresh burst and flowering of faith. And with it, a wider and deeper inner joy than ever experienced before.

But at the very heart of this faith is hardship, endurance, suffering—and Calvary. Without it there cannot be any Christian faith. I have frequently heard my husband remark that Christ willingly gave up His life on the Cross, and that we shall not be able to solve our own great problems until more of us are ready to do likewise.

I think it is the painful idea of Calvary that keeps many

people from seeking the Christian life of faith. Yet everyone is bound to know suffering even without faith and without religion, without church and without prayer, for that is mankind's lot. One cannot escape difficulties and bereavement any more than one can escape death. Purposeless pain, without faith in God, is a tragic waste, a tortuous passageway leading to eternal perdition. With faith all human suffering has a purpose, leading to maturity and fulfillment of one's spirit.

I have spoken of these few outstanding milestones in my own spiritual development chiefly because I think few recognize the awful period of vast bleakness that overcomes an earnest Christian at a testing period. Often the Lord loses some of His best potential followers and faithful soldiers. Feeling deserted, they fall away from their faith and become lost sheep. I wish I could tell each of them individually how worthwhile the testing period is, and how bright the recharging of the spiritual battery can be as one emerges again into the Light with renewed vision.

My crisis hour was in 1949, when China was overrun. After Japan was defeated, and World War II was over, the Chinese Communists donned the cloak of "agrarian reformers," and through smear tactics, character assassinations, infiltrating of the Government, and other devious pressure techniques, succeeded after some three years in forcing my husband to retire as head of the State. Fellow-travelers in the Government and representatives of our former powerful allies made it plain to him that he was an impediment to "peace," and that if only he would retire from office, bloodshed would cease and all obstacles would be obviated. My husband, therefore, despite grave misgivings acquiesced.

The situation deteriorated rapidly, so much so that China's international standing in the winter of 1949 was at its lowest ebb. I was in the United States with the hope that timely aid would save at least a part of the country from the Communists.

Yet after the Generalissimo's retirement news from China continued to grow more fearful. City after city, province after province, fell into Communist hands with rapid succession. The Chinese people felt things had fallen apart. Some army officers, hitherto loyal, defected, taking their troops with them, as Communist propaganda had promised everybody a Utopia on earth. It seemed smart to join the winning side ahead of others, with the attendant result that there was a mad scramble onto the proverbial band wagon. During those chaotic months, the acting head of the government, General Li Tsung-jen, suddenly left for the United States ostensibly for medical treatment. All at once there was no responsible person at the helm of affairs.

Seeing this debacle, my husband, though still without official position, threw himself into salvaging what he could of men and morale. Unfortunately the chaos was complete, and the Government was finally forced to withdraw to Formosa, an island 244 miles in length and seventy-six miles at its widest, not as large as the smallest of our mainland provinces. The world wrote off our China and some of our erstwhile friends and allies recognized the Communist regime on the mainland.

I then determined that no matter what the future held, since I could do no more for my country in America, I would return to share the fate of my husband and my people on Formosa. All my friends tried to dissuade me. They were sure that death awaited my return. They pointed out that my sacrifice would be useless since it was only a matter of weeks, perhaps even days, before Formosa, too, would fall. I felt, however, that life was meaningless if I survived while China perished. How could I let my husband face the greatest set-back of his life without me at his side?

In those dark days, I kept on praying, even though my prayers had become somewhat mechanical and repetitious. Over and over again I would ask my sister, Madame Kung, "How can God allow anything so wicked to happen? How can He allow the Communists to overrun the mainland? Doesn't He know they are His enemies?"

She would reply: "Keep on praying and be patient. I am certain He will open a way."

Then one morning at dawn, unaware whether I was asleep or awake, I heard a Voice—an ethereal Voice saying distinctly:

"*All is right.*"

Fully awakened by the words, I immediately rose and went to my sister's room. She looked up from her bed. She was not surprised by such an early visit because during those troublous days when I was beset with insomnia, I often disturbed her, day or night. Before I could speak, she sat up and said:

"What has happened? Your face looks radiant."

I told her that I had heard God speak to me. This was not the first time in my life that I heard The Voice, for I had other experiences when I was somehow aware of His Presence. I shall not dwell upon them here. Fortunately my sister understood what I meant. When I announced that I was going home by the first available plane, she helped me to pack. No longer did she protest.

Home—to what home was I going? Not to mainland China which I had left over a year ago when our Government and people still had hopes and prospects of defeating the Communist hordes, but to Formosa, a dot on the map. I was going, however, to people who were not duped by the Communists but who had chosen freedom under unbelievably hard and self-abnegating conditions, leaving practically all material things behind them. I was going to my husband, who had flown out of Chungking on one of the last planes, leaving behind him the mainland and part of his heart.

He had reached Formosa only a few weeks earlier in the winter of 1949.

While on the mainland, my husband was everywhere—flying from province to province trying unofficially to stiffen resistance and raise morale. Often I had planned to join him, but it was difficult to keep up with his movements. He would head (for instance) for Shanghai when Shanghai was in peril, and for Canton when Canton's fall was imminent. And thus it went on. He did not know himself where he would be next, nor for how long.

Now with the assurance that "*All is right,*" I was certain that I could join him.

Memories of our perilous days together overwhelmed me

while the airplane motors propelled me toward him and Formosa.

Twenty-eight years ago, when we were married, he had written a moving statement which was published on our wedding day, expressing the goal and aim of what we both hoped to accomplish for China. From that day onward I had tried to the best of my ability to work with him for the achieving of a happy, free, literate, prosperous, and united country.

Much had been accomplished. By military as well as by political means, my husband had worked for the eradication of warlordism, one of the chief scourges which prevented national unity. Together with some of the dedicated men he picked for the Executive Yuan (Cabinet), he planned and opened up the whole country by a system of highways, railways, the gradual improvement of water conservation, and the introduction of airways. For the first time, too, national currency was stabilized under the Finance Minister, Dr. H. H. Kung.

Gradually opium production was eliminated. He worked to build up the nucleus of a modern army in all three services. He succeeded finally in cleaning up large areas of Reds, and the Government had their remnants bottled up in Yen-An. At this psychological moment, Japan, long threatening, had struck. And for eight years China under the Generalissimo staved off the Japanese aggressor, long before the country was prepared to resist.

But the Generalissimo, the government officials, and many others worked on doggedly and oftentimes with great ingenuity "beyond the line of duty." No doubt mistakes were made which, on hindsight, could even be called extremely unwise and fatuous. To preserve a sane equilibrium, the mistakes must be considered along with the stupendous bulldog tenacity and perseverance during the war against Japan which raised China to the status of one of the leading nations of the world, at the end of World War II. I turn sick at heart at the thought of the character assassinations so successfully promoted by the Communists. To the brave patriots who have been slandered, I should like to repeat our old Chinese saying: "When the water recedes, the stones will appear." Nothing remains hidden. Time and God will vindicate them.

During the years after my marriage, I had undergone privations and lived in conditions which I had hitherto never encountered. I had accompanied my husband on his campaigns. We had lived in mud huts, in railway stations, in trains, through the hot stony sandy formations of the Northwest, in primitive barracks, and in tents.

To consolidate his victories I had started schools, orphanages, hospitals, and opium-cure clinics. Everywhere we visited I had enrolled the aid of women and foreign missionaries to reinvigorate or rehabilitate the local people. Together my husband and I had started the National Economic Reconstruction and New Life Movements. I had been interested in promoting a national spoken language to break down our provincial and local barriers of dialects. I had even gone into military service as Secretary General of the Air Force, though my training had been purely in the humanities. Knowing my deficiencies, I was willing to learn. I read up on the subject of aviation and listened to the various Italian and American advisers and experts discussing their experiences in tactical performances and maintenance requirements of the various types of aircraft.

These flash-backs of the past crowded with rapid succession through my mind. Now, while the plane was monotonously droning its way to Formosa, I sat looking out of the rectangular window at my side. I watched cottonly wool clouds coursing swiftly by. Then, suddenly, I asked myself, "*Wherein have I personally failed? Could I have done more?*" At one time we had been within sight of reaching our goal of a truly unified country. *Why had the Communists prevailed?* Question upon question kept firing at me in introspection as the plane kept on its way. *What could I do now?*

The answer occurred to me that while I was trying to live a Christian life and had made some social and political contributions, I had not been working directly for God, under God, and with God. I had been on the periphery of God's guidance, but I had not eliminated self and worked directly *for* Him. Clearly I had been doing things according to Mayling Soong Chiang's light with His help, instead of doing them in God's way with Mayling Soong Chiang as His instrument.

I had been using God, not letting God use me. I had done nothing for Him alone.

An uncertain thought dawned on me as I winged my way across the ocean, that I should perhaps form a prayer group. I had considered myself a Christian recognizing the power of God, but I had failed to make God my motivating and directing force.

I quailed at the thought of a prayer group. I shied away in self-consciousness. My friends would think that I am over-righteous and over-pious, as I had once thought my mother was. Is it not odd that most of us feel no reticence in proclaiming our love for our family and friends, but are most hesitant and embarrassed to let people know of our allegiance to Christ? And since this is true, our devotion to Him withers, for only in reaffirmation can we keep alive love.

I was glad for the plane's stop-overs.

At Manila, as at San Francisco and Honolulu, the tremendous crowd of overseas Chinese who had been waiting since dawn at the airfield to welcome me, moved me deeply. Not only had the older generation turned out in full force, the youths and students down to the last cub scout cheered wildly, waving our Chinese flag. To them I was a symbol of their beloved ancestral land. Any sign that Free China would fight on stirred them deeply. I wonder whether they fully know, our overseas compatriots, how much we love them, and count on them, and how deeply grateful the home-fighters are.

From Manila, I was on the last lap of my journey. How vividly I recall the moment when I sighted the island of Formosa! By prearrangement, the pilot landed me on a small field outside Taipei, for my husband and I wanted a quiet reunion. Contrary to our plans, not only my friends but great crowds had gathered. I greeted my many friends and waved to the crowd that came all the way to wish me well. I was overwhelmed.

Just before my husband and I entered the car, we paused as if by common impulse, and gazed together at the horizon.

Beyond our vision was the mainland. There live five hundred million of our compatriots, enslaved.

We drove to our new home. On this island we would pick up the pieces and rebuild.

Very soon after my arrival in Formosa, I invited five of my friends who were devout Christians and told them that from that day forth I hoped to have a prayer group. I repeated Christ's promise that when two or three are gathered together in His name there He also is. If they agreed, we would pray together for the fate of China and for the world according to His will.

Now a prayer group is nothing new. As I said, my mother held such meetings in our home every week, and after her death, my sister, Madame Kung, faithfully carried on in the old family home. Many prayer-for-peace groups all over the world have recently been started; people seemed to be catching the same religious spark in many parts of the globe. Nearly everyone knows of the astounding world-wide crusades Father Patrick Peyton has been tirelessly making from one corner of the earth to the other, with people signing up for daily family prayer. I firmly believe with him that "the family that prays together, stays together."

Would it not also be true that a nation that prays together, stays together?

My friends were enthusiastic from the start. One of them exclaimed: "This is just what we have been wanting, but somehow never knew!"

Our prayer meeting has been held every Wednesday afternoon without fail for five years. In the beginning, a certain self-consciousness in praying aloud had to be overcome. We were somewhat abashed at the start. Some of us had never prayed aloud. People who have known each other intimately can suddenly seem strangers in the presence of God. But there comes a moment when God takes over and the Holy Spirit is really with us.

We take turns in leading the meeting, for faith increases with frequency of public affirmation. We usually start with two minutes of silent prayer followed by singing some well-loved hymns. The leader reads from the Scriptures and tells of her own spiritual testimony in relation to the lesson. After that comes open discussion on the subject. Then members request prayers for particular reasons or people. Reverently we kneel, and one at a time pray as the Spirit moves us. Three or four prayers are offered. There is no rigid schedule; we feel that spontaneity and diversity are conducive to enthusiasm.

As time went on, the prayer group enlarged its membership. The constituency changed and broadened. We pledge only one thing: unless prevented by serious illness or by unavoidable circumstances (such as absence from the city), we would attend. We see to it that other engagements do not conflict with this set-apart period.

There are forty members in this group, far more than we originally planned. We have struggled to keep it small; it is hard not to take in the many who would like to join us. An intimate feeling of unity and informality can only be had if not too many people are present. Branches headed by our members are all over the city. We have a joint meeting of all these groups once every three months.

Starting with six earnest Christians, we began to take in lukewarm believers; then others who had some knowledge of Christianity but had never been baptized. Gradually all of these, helped by a study class, became professed practicing Christians. We were careful not to dilute the faith, and so worked slowly.

Suddenly we found we were accepting women who were without any Christian or religious interest. This is how it came about. At one meeting the leader spoke of the difference between communism and Christianity in the method of propaganda. She stated that whenever Communists spot a person with qualities of outstanding leadership they go after her and work on her until she is added to the ring of Communist workers. Their work is successful because of the kind of people they pick. Christians do not seem to pick outstanding converts to enforce their ranks. Should not we carefully select those of unusual ability or influence to promote Christianity?

After the general discussion, I felt moved to sum up our conclusions, "There is a great deal of truth in what you said. But the difference between communism and Christianity lies in this: communism in practice has shown itself interested in strengthening the Communist State at the expense of the human being, who is expendable to the cause, whereas Christ came into the world for the whole as well as for the sick, for the saintly as well as for the sinner. Christianity's concern is for the salvation of the individual, and the individual soul is all-important to God. He chose Paul and Luke; Nicodemus and Joseph of Arimathea could not resist Him. These were men of education, intelligence, and position. But Christ also chose the illiterate fisherman, the lowly tax gatherer.

"None of us can do much by ourselves. Men are spiritually powerful either through the work of the devil or the Holy Spirit. Purity of heart is found in both the intellectual and the lowly. God finds His own tools anywhere, everywhere. With Him there are no pariahs. Did not Christ say: 'Go out into the highways and hedges, and compel them to come in, that my house may be filled.'?"*

As a result one of the members came to me after the meeting and told me of a non-Christian friend sorely in need of help. This woman had lost her whole family of six children. A few months ago, a ship coming to Formosa, on which her last surviving son was aboard, sank. Every one of the thousand-odd aboard was drowned. The mother almost lost her mind. She would not believe her boy was really dead. Later, when our troops withdrew from Chusan Island, she stood on the wharf for three days and nights as each ship came in, her eyes straining at the face of every soldier filing down the gangplank from the ships. She kept asking, "Do you know a man by the name of Yeh I-kun? Was he in your outfit?" When the last ship was unloaded, she gazed for a long time at the unfeeling ocean which had taken her child. Returning home, she tried to kill herself. Nothing would comfort her. She sat with a vacuous stare, huddled in silence.

* Luke 14:23.

When this woman was brought to our meeting, we all showed her our concern and sympathy. We prayed with her that God would comfort and sustain all whose hearts were breaking through bereavement. Some wept with her. . . .

To our amazement, she returned voluntarily without urging. Her mind cleared. Within a year after she joined the group, she was baptized. It is not often that one hears prayers so powerful, so beautiful, and so filled with God's grace as hers. She converted her eighty-year-old mother-in-law, a devout Buddhist, to Christianity. The old lady, just before her death, stipulated to her family that she wanted a Christian burial, forbidding the usual elaborate Buddhist rites.

Since that wonderful experience, we have been taking those who need God regardless of their mental or religious attitudes.

Earlier with the group, I experienced what I had so often heard about and never quite understood: spiritual joy and exhilaration. Very soon I realized that others were feeling the same. This is the fruit of a prayer group: intellectual conviction in the proofs all around them of the power of prayer plus an entirely fresh suffusion of inward joy. Here is the key to one of the swiftest ways religion becomes truly personal. "The fruit of the Spirit is love, joy, peace, long suffering, gentleness, goodness, faith, meekness, temperance. . . ."*

As I have said, I have been long convinced intellectually of a Supreme Being. All nature pointed to it; all science affirmed it. But God to me had been an impersonal power and heretofore I flinched from anything *mystique.* I did not go so far in Hu-

* Galatians 5:22.

manitarianism as its distinctive tenet of denying the Divinity of Christ. Universal laws readily enough point to a Supreme Intelligence. But one does not *love* a Supreme Intelligence, a Universal Truth, or a Divine Law. Not until God becomes a loving Father intimately concerned with your personal problems are you able to love the Lord your God with your heart, your mind, and your soul.

And this is how I began to get the gradual feeling of love for God. One day, three years ago, while reading of the Crucifixion, I paused at a passage where the soldier used a spear to pierce His side, causing blood and water to flow from the wound. I had read that passage many times before, and it had never particularly moved me. This time, however, I wept. At last I felt that the suffering and pain of Jesus Christ were for me. I cried and cried, overcome with my own unworthiness.

It was a peculiar sensation, at once great grief and great release. I can count the times I have wept since I have grown up, for as children we were taught not to show emotion, and to abhor sentimentality. How well I remember my father, suddenly turning stern and seemingly unapproachable, when I sobbed and wailed because my elder brother, T. V., left home for the first time to attend boarding school. Now my tears were a torrent. I could not control myself. At the same time, my heart felt light and relieved, with a sense of atonement. I think I experienced what is called an old-fashioned conversion. No other word will do. Thenceforth I was not only convinced in mind, but I felt a very strong immanence of God. The passage, "If any man be in Christ he is a new creature; old things are passed away; behold all things are become new"* took on new meaning.

When I told of this to a few of our group, some instantly understood and recognized what I tried to convey. (Conversion is very difficult to explain, except to those who have been through it.)

Loving-thy-neighbor-as-thyself became very real to us. Whether or not we are intimate friends, a dear bond is formed in praying together. Each of us feel exultation and joy whenever we hear that an almost impossible problem is happily solved through prayer. There is an odd spiritual excitement when an unbeliever becomes a Christian and is baptized. We do not ask nor care to what church denominations we belonged. We know there are nominal Buddhists and atheists among us, but we feel that God's design brought them to us and will convert them.

As time progressed, our members formed other prayer groups among their own friends without our urging. Some of these consist of married couples. A member who moved away from the city of Taipei started one in her own village. Still another, while undergoing further professional training, started one among her fellow students.

Before speaking more of my own prayer group, I should like to tell you of other groups not directly connected with us and some of their experiences. To our actual knowledge, there are over one hundred such groups in Free China, but there may well be many others. Stories come back to us of changed lives quite as incredible as those that have happened to our own unit,

* II Corinthians 5:17.

and these include numerous healings and recoveries from illnesses and shock considered incurable. Frankly, when I am ill, I pray to God to guide my doctors. I have often heard it said that not until a case is considered hopeless do people beget enough faith for miracle cures. I think this is true.

One story particularly interested me because I knew the person and her problems. She had an adolescent son going wild, seriously so, in secret bad company. She started family prayers against the protests of her own children. But she kept on, and now the wayward son is a fine, filial boy. The change in him is phenomenal.

A certain woman had remained behind on the mainland to care for her husband's ailing parents who were too old to travel when he came to Formosa, just before the mainland was lost. She was risking her life in being so faithful. The old couple died, and she herself was thrown into a concentration camp. Several years later she managed to escape, and succeeded in her flight to Free China only to find that her husband, having been mistakenly informed that she, too, had died, had re-married. Her bitterness, his remorse, and the stunned bewilderment of the other woman, had the makings of tragedy. Finally, through earnest prayers, the second woman, who is a Christian, voluntarily relinquished all claims, and is now devoting herself to her former profession as a teacher.

A man noted for his love of gambling joined a prayer group, and since then gradually has lost the urge for the excitement of the gambler's life. Prayers and the prayer group made him realize that the stimulation stemmed from covetousness, while he had thought he was only seeking a thrill, which he had considered a natural enough human inclination.

A morphine addict did not have the will-power nor the desire to cure himself of the habit, although his family had been made destitute through his indulgence. One day as he was passing a friend's house, he decided to go in. A prayer meeting was just beginning, and because of urgings, he sat down. "Something extraordinary happened to me during the meeting," he said later in telling of his conversion, "I don't know what. All of a sudden I realized that I was plunging my family into ruin, and that I held the stewardship from God for each soul in my family. I decided then and there that with God's help I would stop using morphine." He has kept his pledge, and that was two years ago.

A week after the Tachen evacuation, one of the refugees came to my office. He was an old man, a shopkeeper. He and his wife for a long time had been the only Christians on Tachen. There never has been a clergyman there. Alone they had converted over five hundred people! Two years ago, our prayer group sent them some Bibles as a gift. Since then, every Wednesday at the same hour that we hold meetings, some sixty Christians in Tachen had met to pray. When the Government offered to evacuate the Tachen population, this shopkeeper donated everything in his store to the armed forces. He and his family came over with nothing except a few bundles. When asked about his future, he replied confidently, "The Lord will provide."

When he finished, it was just about time for our Wednesday prayer meeting. I invited him to share his story and to pray with us. He said shyly that he had had only a month's schooling in all his life, but that he could read the New Testament except for five or six words, and could recite many portions from memory. To our amazement, not only was his prayer deeply spiritual, but his language was that of an educated man.

Many years ago, my sister, Madame Kung, had a friend who was such a devout Buddhist that she had established a nunnery on a beautiful mountain in Hangchow. She planned to spend the rest of her life there, for she had divorced her husband and had no children. Madame Kung tried for many years to interest her in Christianity, but whenever she accompanied my sister to our old family home in Shanghai for the weekly prayer meeting, she would take along her knitting and remain in the library while the meeting was in progress. She wanted none of it.

But after six years she was converted. She is now a member of our original prayer group. When her husband, who was immensely wealthy, died, his estate, due to complicated financial deals, was a problem to his family. They sought her help, and although she had long been divorced, she helped them to clear it up. Immensely grateful, the family told her that she could have any part of the estate she wanted.

"When I divorced him," she replied, "I would not take a cent; and now that he is dead, I want nothing. If I had been a Christian, I would never have left him. Who knows what prayer might have done for him? If you insist, I should like the share that you offer me to be used as a foundation fund for scholarships and for a home for orphans dedicated to his memory."

Today there are sixty scholarships in memory of him in Formosa. The orphanage is the best run in Free China. This friend of my sister who did not have a child of her own is instrumental in raising many children for God.

Nothing comes easily, however. Before she succeeded, she underwent much discouragement. When the orphanage was first started the Board of Trustees (of which she, as the founder, was a member), selected a superintendent who mishandled the job. As he had been recommended by many members of the deceased's family, the founder did not want any conflict over him. Yet she felt deeply distressed for the children. For a year and a half she prayed with us for a solution. Finally a way was opened for the superintendent's resignation without bitterness on anyone's part. The orphanage conditions were then clear to all, and the deceased's family begged the founder to right them. She herself took over the administration and instituted Christian training. Yet all that took long earnest prayer. We have learned that too many give up praying after the first burst of fervor.

Strangely enough some lives are changed in an instant, and some problems are solved miraculously. Just as Paul's conversion was an instantaneous call, so occasionally is a conversion among us. Others seem to have to storm the doors of heaven. This has often puzzled me. Why should some receive spiritual help and gifts immediately, often without conscious volition or desire on their part, while others, including myself, are constantly struggling? I have had to learn to rest content with the knowledge that God has a divine plan, and "works in a mysterious way." Newman must have been puzzled so, when he wrote in that beautiful hymn, *Lead Kindly Light,* "one step enough for me."

Sometimes even firm Christians forget certain fundamentals; to avoid that, we prepared a pamphlet with the Ten Commandments, the Lord's Prayer, the Beatitudes, and the Apostles' Creed, which we memorize for spiritual help in our private meditations. We all find that learning a favorite Bible verse and repeating it at odd moments during the day provides the material needed to practice the presence of God. Otherwise we are destitute in contemplation of Him.

Our original intention, if you remember, was to pray for the country and for God's will among nations. This we did with regularity, but soon an innate feeling demanded that faith multiply through us. We began evangelical work among the armed forces. In the beginning we put chaplains in the military hospitals and later in the army.

For the first time in history China now has a chaplain service. Eleven trained full-time chaplains do bedside visiting among the sick and the wounded and hold regular Christian services. This project is supported by the voluntary tithing of our members, and by contributions of Madame Kung and her friends. Prayer group members make weekly visits to military hospitals. This is not merely social or welfare service; it is definitely doing God's work and furthering His Word. It is said that "He who teaches a prayer, prays in many voices." Our group knows that hundreds, even thousands of prayers would never have been offered without us. We have had grateful letters not only from the soldiers themselves, but from the hospital authorities.

But do not think we had smooth sailing. Anyone who has tried to spread His Word knows the impediments, the sharp rocks that lie on the path. And everyone knows the pernickety red-tape that abounds in government organizations everywhere in the world. Time and again the work has been obstructed, as though by the devil himself. But we persisted. The results are heartening.

Consider what some of our wounded soldiers and officers have been through. They fought the Japanese, then the Communists, only to be withdrawn from the mainland. Most of them have no idea where and how their families are faring; others have heard of the tortures and death of their loved ones left behind. Many of them are sick in body and mind, feeling betrayed from within and given up from without by our erstwhile allies. Too often officers and men would commit suicide together soon after they reached the hospital. But since 1950, in those hospitals where our chaplains went into action, there has not been one suicide.

In the hospitals alone our latest record shows four thousand three hundred and twenty baptisms.

On Christmas Eve, four thousand Christians led by our prayer group met at Taipei City Hall to celebrate the birth of Christ. The hall was crowded and thousands outside listened to loudspeakers. Soon after, many requests to join a prayer group came to us.

On Easter, our prayer group leads Good Friday services which are broadcast. The beauty and poignancy of Christ's message have been felt by many who formerly were not Christians.

We stress that after the crucifixion of Christ, with the exception of Judas Iscariot (who in remorse and shame hanged himself) the eleven simple ordinary men became veritable spiritual giants, developing amazing qualities of leadership. They were tortured and persecuted, yet they continued to proclaim the gospel. Of them all, John was the only one who died a natural death. The rest were all martyred, and Peter, whose fear had once caused him to deny Christ three times, was later nailed to a cross upside down, at his own request. Even doubting Thomas staked his life on the Faith.

With these men, latent possibilities evolved into certainties. Selfishness was transformed into selflessness. Instead of scattering like lost sheep without a shepherd, this small handful of Christians became an invincible unit despite formidable oppression and persecution. The meager band of believers proved to be, in time, a more potent force than the entire Roman Empire. They became Divine instruments and were truly the founding fathers of the early Christian church, which has prevailed nearly two thousand years.

Today's tendency is to think ourselves rationalists. It has been the Communist technique to rob us of our faith. Part of the devil's cunning has seared us with cowardice, cynicism, compromise, indifference, false standards, and irresponsibility. For too long has this been the state of mind of many of us. Within us are mental and spiritual road-blocks which must be removed if we are to progress.

Many Christians of the present generation have become confused and have lacked the spiritual fire to *insist* on a better world. World War II demonstrated in blood and agony that an apathetic people is an invitation to totalitarianism. We can have a better world only if we care enough.

Once when my husband spoke to his officers, he said: "I am worried for you. It is important for all of you whether you have any religious faith and whatever your religious faith may be, to recognize the indisputable existence of the Arbiter—God. He is in the hearts of all men. This is in keeping with our Chinese philosophy 'unity between heaven and man.' "

In all efforts there is bound to be some disillusionment. We dream higher than we build. We look for immediate and dazzling success, and when it doesn't come, gloom or pessimism takes its place. In some quarters men have been lulled by the opiate of too easy success. We forget that often great success comes to us in the shadow of apparent failure.

Many years ago, I made a trip to Zose in Tsin-poo county, a scenic spot near Shanghai. From the bottom of the hill, a long ascent of stone steps led to a half-way rest. From this point to the summit there were fourteen turns illustrating the journey of Christ along the Via Dolorosa, with a Bible verse pointing out the lesson to be learned from that stage of our Saviour's last journey. At the crest of the hill rose a beautiful cathedral—the summation of the meaning of the Cross—the symbol of human suffering and Divine atonement.

Truly, it was an inspiring sight. Yet to one unfamiliar with Christ, these fourteen plaques told the story of a dismal failure. It would seem that Christ's mission had ended in unrelieved disaster. We who are privileged know that His career was the greatest triumph in all history. He changed civilization.

In moments of disillusionment and disappointment, the memory of that scenic, holy spot reminds me of how infinitesimally small and trifling individual human disappointments are, and how infinite is His love. And I am reinvigorated with added inner strength to face the future. God's great and universal love has not rendered me fainthearted and fazed towards atheistic communism. For is not the Christian church on earth the church militant engaged in constant warfare against its enemies, the powers of evil?

Christ was no appeaser. He spoke, but He also acted. He lashed out against "Ye generation of vipers." He took a whip in His hand and used it against those who defiled His Father's house. What could truly prevent man's descent to bestiality and abomination were conscience destroyed and the ultimate accounting to God taught to be non-existent?

Many people shudder at the thought of atonement, just as they shudder at the thought of the Cross. But atonement or retribution there will be. We must make a choice.

Atonement before God has a purpose and a meaning, adding stature to the soul. Retribution involves inflicted suffering of our loved ones, sooner or later. Those who break God's laws pay the price to the third or fourth generation.

Science teaches us that every action has a consequence. So does the past. There is no escape. This inexorable law goes further: we can sin and cause evil by what we do. We can also sin and cause evil by what we leave undone. Much of today's chaos is the consequence of sins of omission. We so often ask, why should the innocent suffer? We so seldom ask, what have I left undone to cause innocent people to suffer?

The four gospels record that throughout His ministry Christ frequently had to get away from the multitudes to commune with His Father not only by Himself, but together with His band of disciples. He, the Son of God, needed to recharge His spirit by prayer. How much more do we need prayer!

This is what we must have and must have quickly: a chain of prayer groups around the world; a turning to God of all those who call themselves Christians and who will welcome amongst them those who have no spiritual home.

Civilization will advance in proportion to the personal concern, enthusiasm, and faith through prayer that we soak into it. Then will be sure victory.

天 之 道